Table of Contents   Cursive

Table of Contents, continued   Cursive

About This Book

This *Spectrum® Cursive Handwriting* workbook provides the support your child needs to master handwriting in cursive form. Lessons demonstrate proper formation of both uppercase and lowercase letters and provide practice in writing individual letters, letter combinations, words, and sentences.

Lowercase letters are taught first because they are generally simpler to form than uppercase letters and occur more often in writing. The lessons within each chapter are ordered based on the hand movements used to write in cursive.

t i u w	simple upward strokes
c a d q g o	counter-clockwise curves
r s j p	complex upward strokes
n m v x y z	humps
e l b h k f	loops
C A O E	counter-clockwise curves
U W V Y	downward curves
X Z Q	complex curves
P B R N M	downward strokes with humps
H K T F	multi-step sticks and hooks
I J D L G S	loops

Chapter 1 introduces each lowercase letter, and **Chapter 2** introduces each uppercase letter. Guiding arrows are provided to help with proper letter formation.

t tt

In **Chapter 3**, students gain exposure to content-area vocabulary while they practice. Words are pulled from grades 3–5 math, language arts, science, and social studies vocabulary lists.

In the **Final Review**, students copy silly sentences that contain all 26 letters of the alphabet and then compose an **A–Z** sentence of their own. The **Final Test** is to write a letter to a friend in cursive. This assesses not only correct letter formation but the ability to fluidly write one's own original thoughts.

Aa Bb Cc Dd Ee

Ff Gg Hh Ii Jj

Kk Ll Mm Nn

Oo Pp Qq Rr

Ss Tt Uu Vv

Ww Xx Yy Zz

Aa Bb Cc Dd Ee

Ff Gg Hh Ii Jj

Kk Ll Mm Nn

Oo Pp Qq Rr

Ss Tt Uu Vv

Ww Xx Yy Zz

Try writing in cursive. Use words for your age.

Full Name: _____

Address: _____

Age: _____

Date: _____

Cursive Basics

Writing in cursive involves different skills than writing in manuscript. Here are some basics to keep in mind.

- Because letters connect with each other, you must practice making your writing flow across the page.
- Cursive is written at a slant instead of straight up and down. To make it easy to write with a slant, tilt the page.

Left-handed writers should tilt the page so that the lower right corner points toward them.

Right-handed writers should tilt the page so that the lower left corner points toward them.

- Where a letter begins is important. Make sure you write in the correct direction, as shown by the arrow(s) on each new letter in this book, even when connnecting letters together. For most letters, this means you will follow the connecting line to the usual starting point of the letter. You may have to backtrack over your work.

Starting Point

- Some uppercase letters connect to other letters in a word, and some do not. Pay special attention to this when learning uppercase letters.

- When writing lowercase letters, wait until all letters in a word are formed before going back to add any dots or crosses. In fact, you should only lift your pencil from the page in these three cases:

    1. between words

    2. after uppercase letters that do not connect

    3. when forming uppercase letters that have more than one step

    Note: In this book, if there is more than one movement required for a letter, steps will be numbered. You may see an arrow, a cross, or a dot with a number next to it.

Cursive Tips

Follow these simple tips to make it easier to learn to write in cursive.

- Use a sharp pencil, not a pen, to practice your cursive. It is much easier to control a pencil than a pen. Plus, you can erase mistakes and try again.

- After every few words, stop and check that your paper is still turned so that your writing stays slanted.

- After learning all letters, practice starting words with a lowercase letter and then with an uppercase letter. This will help make the connection between the two letter forms.

- Think about how to spell a word before you begin writing it. This will help you keep your writing fluid.

- Practice reading cursive, too. You might ask a teacher or parent to write to you in cursive. The more you read cursive, the easier it will become to write.

- Write in cursive for 20 minutes every day. It's okay if you don't do it perfectly. The more you practice, the better you will get, and the less likely you'll be to forget how to form certain letters.

- Learn cursive with a friend. Then, you can practice by writing notes to each other. You could even use it as a secret code that your printing friends can't understand!

Lowercase **t**

Trace and write.

(cursive handwriting practice rows of lowercase letter t and tt)

Lesson 1.2   Lowercase i

Trace and write.

i i i i i

i i i i i

i i i i i

ii ii ii ii ii

ii ii ii ii

it it it it it

it it it it it

ti ti ti ti ti

ti ti ti

ti ti ti

Lesson 1.3   Lowercase u

Trace and write.

u u u u u

u u u u

u u u u

ui ui ui ui ui

ui ui ui ui ui

ut ut ut ut ut

ut ut ut ut

tu tu tu tu tu

tu tu tu

tu tu tu

NAME _____

Trace and write.

w w w w w

wi wi wi wi wi

ww ww ww ww ww

tw tw tw tw tw

Review Lessons 1.1-1.4 | Lowercase **t**, **i**, **u**, and **w**

Trace and write.

tt   ii   it   ut   tu

tu   ui   uu   ut   ti

tut   uit

Lesson 1.5   Lowercase **c**

Trace and write.

Lesson 1.6   Lowercase a

Trace and write.

a   *a*   *a*   *a*   *a*

at   *at*   *at*   *ta*   *ta*

ai   *ai*   *ai*   *ia*   *ia*

aw   *aw*   *aw*   *wa*   *wa*

ac   *ac*   *ca*   *ca*

Lesson 1.7   Lowercase **d**

Trace and write.

d d d d d

dd dd dd dd dd

di di di di di

id id du du du

da da ad ad

Lesson 1.8 Lowercase **q**

Trace and write.

q q q q q

qu qu qu qu qu

cq cq cq cq cq

aq aq aq aq aq

Lesson 1.9 Lowercase **g**

Trace and write.

$\bar{g}$ g g g g

gg gg gg gg gg

gi gi gi ig ig

ug ug ug gu gu

ag ag ga ga

Lesson 1.10 Lowercase o

Trace and write.

ō   o   o   o   o

oi   oi   oi   io   io

to   to   to   ou   ou

ou   ou   oc   co   co

od   od   do   do

Review Lessons 1.5–1.10 | Lowercase **c**, **a**, **d**, **q**, **g**, and **o**

Trace and write.

tic   *cut*   *cou*

act   *dad*   *wad*

cat   *tad*   *toad*

coat   *data*   *auto*

Review Lessons 1.5–1.10 Lowercase **c**, **a**, **d**, **q**, **g**, and **o**

Trace and write.

tag   *tug*   *quit*

wag   *wig*   *twig*

goat   *quit*   *aqua*

quad   *quo*   *odd*

Lesson 1.11   Lowercase r

Trace and write.

r   *r*   *r*   *r*   *r*

ri   *ri*   *rt*   *tr*   *tr*

rd   *rd*   *dr*   *dr*   *dr*

ro   *ro*   *ro*   *or*   *or*

ra   *ra*   *ar*   *ar*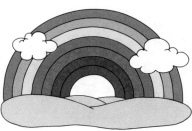

Lesson 1.12 · Lowercase s

Trace and write.

s s s s s

ss ss ss ss ss

st si su sur sc

sa ts so is us

ws ds gs cs

Lesson 1.13   Lowercase **j**

Trace and write.

j   *j*   *j*   *j*   *j*

ji   *ji*   *ji*   *ji*   *ji*

ju   *ju*   *ju*   *ju*   *ju*

ja   *ja*   *ja*   *ja*   *ja*

jo   *jo*   *jo*   *jo*

Lesson 1.14   Lowercase **p**

Trace and write.

p   *p*   *p*   *p*   *p*

pp   *pp*   *pp*   *pt*   *pt*

pi   *pi*   *pu*   *up*   *up*

pa   *pa*   *ap*   *po*   *op*

ps   *sp*   *sp*   *pr*

Review Lessons 1.11–1.14 Lowercase **r**, **s**, **j**, and **p**

Trace and write.

rap stop jig

pairs soar jugs

road drop art

proud stow poor

roads pats jaguar

Lesson 1.15 Lowercase **n**

Trace and write.

n   *n*   *n*   *n*   *n*

nn   *nt*   *ni*   *in*   *in*

na   *an*   *an*   *no*   *no*

nd   *nd*   *ng*   *ng*   *gn*

ns   *ns*   *nu*   *un*

Lesson 1.16 Lowercase **m**

Trace and write.

m   *m*   *m*   *m*   *m*

mm   *mm*   *mi*   *im*

mu   *um*   *ma*   *am*

mo   *om*   *ms*   *ms*

sm   *mp*   *rm*

Lesson 1.17 Lowercase **v**

Trace and write.

v　　v　　v　　v　　v

vi　　vi　　vi　　iv　　iv

va　　va　　va　　av　　av

vo　　vo　　ov　　ov　　vw

Lesson 1.18   Lowercase **x**

Trace and write.

x   x   x   x   x

xi   xi   ix   ix   ix

xt   xt   xt   ux   ux

ax   ax   ox   ox   xy

Lesson 1.19 Lowercase **y**

Trace and write.

y   y   y   y   y

ty   cy   cy   ay   ay

ya   ya   yo   yo   yo

dy   dy   oy   oy   ry

sy   my   py

Lesson 1.20 Lowercase **z**

Trace and write.

z *z* *z* *z* *z*

zy *zy* *zy* *zy* *zy*

ze *ze* *ze* *ze* *ze*

za *za* *za* *az* *az*

zi *zi* *iz* *iz*

Review Lessons 1.15–1.20 Lowercase **n**, **m**, **v**, **x**, **y**, and **z**

Trace and write.

not   *may*   *gnat*

mom   *man*   *mud*

mommy   *moan*

van   *vary*   *savor*

Review Lessons 1.15–1.20 Lowercase n, m, v, x, y, and z

Trace and write.

any many yams

ivy vex victory

tax pox yak

zip zoo crazy

Lesson 1.21　Lowercase **e**

Trace and write.

e　*e*　*e*　*e*　*e*

ei　*ie*　*ea*　*ee*　*te*

eu　*ed*　*ed*　*es*　*es*

er　*er*　*re*　*re*　*we*

en　*me*　*er*　*ey*

Lesson 1.22　Lowercase l

Trace and write.

l   *l*   *l*   *l*   *l*

ll   *ll*   *li*   *il*   *lt*

lo   *ol*   *la*   *la*   *al*

sl   *ls*   *rl*   *ly*   *ly*

el   *el*   *le*   *le*

Lesson 1.23 Lowercase **b**

Trace and write.

b   *b*   *b*   *b*   *b*

bb   *bi*   *bu*   *ba*   *ba*

bo   *bo*   *bo*   *ob*   *ob*

br   *rb*   *bs*   *bs*   *mb*

by   *be*   *be*   *bt*

Lesson 1.24 Lowercase **h**

Trace and write.

h   *h*   *h*   *h*   *h*

hi   *hi*   *th*   *th*   *hu*

ch   *ch*   *ha*   *gh*   *gh*

ho   *oh*   *ov*   *ov*   *ro*

sh   *ph*   *he*   *he*

Lesson 1.25   Lowercase **k**

Trace and write.

k   *k*   *k*   *k*   *k*

ki   *ki*   *ki*   *wk*   *wk*

ck   *ck*   *ck*   *ok*   *ok*

rk   *rk*   *ks*   *ks*   *nk*

ky   *ke*   *ke*   *lk*

Lesson 1.26 Lowercase **f**

Trace and write.

Review Lessons 1.21–1.26 Lowercase **e**, **l**, **b**, **h**, **k**, and **f**

Trace and write.

elf   *fall*   *elbow*

light   *blue*   *black*

lily   *belt*   *brick*

hello   *hunk*   *hefty*

Review Lessons 1.21–1.26 Lowercase **e**, **l**, **b**, **h**, **k**, and **f**

Trace and write.

key   kite   monkey

chunk   shelf   thief

sheep   shift   fake

thick   ache   flight

Review

Trace and write.

Spectrum Cursive Handwriting
Grades 3–5
44

Lesson 2.2   Uppercase **A**

Trace and write.

a   a   a   a   a

Ai   Ai   At   At   At

Ac   Ac   Ar   Ar   Ar

Am   Am   An   An   An

Af   Af   At   At   At

Lesson 2.3 Uppercase O

Trace and write.

O _____ *O* _____ *O* _____ *O* _____ *O*

Ot __ *Ot* __ *Ot* __ *Ou* __ *Ou*

Ok __ *Ok* __ *Om* __ *Om*

Or __ *Or* __ *Or* __ *Op* __ *Op*

Od __ *Od* __ *Ot* __ *Ot* __ *Ot*

Lesson 2.4 Uppercase **E**

Trace and write.

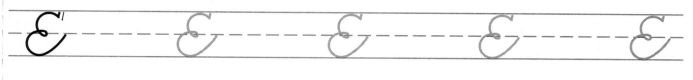

$\mathcal{E}$ $\mathcal{E}$ $\mathcal{E}$ $\mathcal{E}$ $\mathcal{E}$

$\mathcal{E}u$ $\mathcal{E}u$ $\mathcal{E}a$ $\mathcal{E}a$ $\mathcal{E}a$

$\mathcal{E}q$ $\mathcal{E}q$ $\mathcal{E}q$ $\mathcal{E}c$ $\mathcal{E}c$

$\mathcal{E}r$ $\mathcal{E}r$ $\mathcal{E}m$ $\mathcal{E}m$ $\mathcal{E}m$

$\mathcal{E}r$ $\mathcal{E}r$ $\mathcal{E}l$ $\mathcal{E}l$ $\mathcal{E}l$

Uppercase **C**, **A**, **O**, and **E**

NAME _____

Review

Chicago

Arizona

Oregon

Earth

Oregon

Lesson 2.5   Uppercase **U**

Trace and write.

U   *U*   *U*   *U*   *U*

Un   *Un*   *Un*   *Un*   *Un*

Ut   *Ut*   *Ut*   *Ut*   *Ut*

Ur   *Ur*   *Ur*   *Ur*   *Ur*

Um   *Um*   *Uk*   *Uk*

Lesson 2.6   Uppercase **W**

Trace and write.

$\mathcal{W}$ $\mathcal{W}$ $\mathcal{W}$ $\mathcal{W}$ $\mathcal{W}$

$\mathcal{Wi}$ $\mathcal{Wi}$ $\mathcal{Wi}$ $\mathcal{Wi}$ $\mathcal{Wi}$

$\mathcal{Wa}$ $\mathcal{Wa}$ $\mathcal{Wa}$ $\mathcal{Wa}$ $\mathcal{Wa}$

$\mathcal{Wo}$ $\mathcal{Wo}$ $\mathcal{Wo}$ $\mathcal{Wo}$ $\mathcal{Wo}$

$\mathcal{We}$ $\mathcal{We}$ $\mathcal{We}$ $\mathcal{We}$ $\mathcal{We}$

Lesson 2.7 Uppercase **V**

Trace and write.

$\mathcal{V}$ $\mathcal{V}$ $\mathcal{V}$ $\mathcal{V}$ $\mathcal{V}$

$\mathcal{Vi}$ $\mathcal{Vi}$ $\mathcal{Vi}$ $\mathcal{Vi}$ $\mathcal{Vi}$

$\mathcal{Vo}$ $\mathcal{Vo}$ $\mathcal{Vo}$ $\mathcal{Vo}$ $\mathcal{Vo}$

$\mathcal{Va}$ $\mathcal{Va}$ $\mathcal{Va}$ $\mathcal{Va}$ $\mathcal{Va}$

$\mathcal{Ve}$ $\mathcal{Ve}$ $\mathcal{Ve}$ $\mathcal{Ve}$ $\mathcal{Ve}$

Lesson 2.8   Uppercase **Y**

Trace and write.

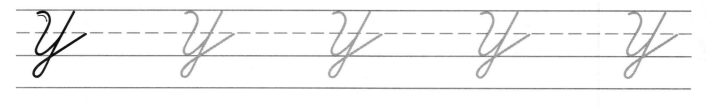

Review Lessons 2.5-2.8 — Uppercase **U**, **W**, **V**, and **Y**

Trace and write.

Utah

Wisconsin

Venus

Yosemite

Review

Yosemite

Lesson 2.9   Uppercase **X**

Trace and write.

𝒳 𝒳 𝒳 𝒳 𝒳

𝒳-n 𝒳-n 𝒳-n 𝒳-n

𝒳i 𝒳i 𝒳i 𝒳i 𝒳i

𝒳a 𝒳a 𝒳a 𝒳a 𝒳a

𝒳e 𝒳e 𝒳e 𝒳e 𝒳e

Lesson 2.10 Uppercase **Z**

Trace and write.

Z   Z   Z   Z   Z

Za   Za   Za   Za   Za

Zo   Zo   Zo   Zo   Zo

Zi   Zi   Zi   Zi   Zi

Ze   Ze   Ze   Ze   Ze

Lesson 2.11 Uppercase **Q**

Trace and write.

Review Lessons 2.9–2.11 Uppercase **X**, **Z**, and **Q**

Trace and write.

Xavier

Zambia

Zelda

Quincy

Lesson 2.12 Uppercase **P**

Trace and write.

P   P   P   P   P

Pa   Pa   Pa   Pa   Pa

Pr   Pr   Pr   Pr   Pr

Pu   Pu   Pu   Pu   Pu

Pe   Pe   Po   Po   Po

Lesson 2.13 Uppercase **B**

Trace and write.

Lesson 2.14 Uppercase **R**

Trace and write.

R   R   R   R   R

Re   Re   Re   Re   Re

Ro   Ro   Ro   Ro   Ro

Ra   Ra   Ra   Ra   Ra

Ri   Ri   Ri   Ru   Ru

Review Lessons 2.12–2.14

Uppercase **P**, **B**, and **R**

Trace and write.

Puerto Rico

Belgium

Reagan

NAME _____

Trace and write.

N   *N*   *N*   *N*   *N*

Na   *Na*   *Na*   *Na*   *Na*

No   *No*   *No*   *No*   *No*

Ne   *Ne*   *Ne*   *Ne*   *Ne*

Ni   *Ni*   *Ni*   *Ni*   *Ni*

Lesson 2.16 Uppercase **M**

Trace and write.

m m m m m

Ma Ma Ma Ma Ma

Mo Mo Mo Mo Mo

Mi Mi Mi Mi Mi

Me Me My My My

Lesson 2.17 Uppercase **H**

Trace and write.

(cursive practice lines: uppercase H)

(cursive practice lines: He He He He He)

(cursive practice lines: Ha Ha Ha Ha Ha)

(cursive practice lines: Ho Ho Ho Ho Ho)

(cursive practice lines: Hu Hu Hu Hu Hu)

Lesson 2.18 Uppercase **K**

Trace and write.

$\mathcal{K}$ $\mathcal{K}$ $\mathcal{K}$ $\mathcal{K}$ $\mathcal{K}$

$\mathcal{K}a$ $\mathcal{K}a$ $\mathcal{K}a$ $\mathcal{K}a$ $\mathcal{K}a$

$\mathcal{K}o$ $\mathcal{K}o$ $\mathcal{K}o$ $\mathcal{K}o$ $\mathcal{K}o$

$\mathcal{K}e$ $\mathcal{K}e$ $\mathcal{K}e$ $\mathcal{K}e$ $\mathcal{K}e$

$\mathcal{K}i$ $\mathcal{K}i$ $\mathcal{K}i$ $\mathcal{K}i$ $\mathcal{K}i$

Review Lessons 2.15–2.18 | Uppercase **N**, **M**, **H**, and **K**

Review

Trace and write.

New Mexico

Missouri

Hawaii

Key West

☆
SANTA FE

New Mexico

Lesson 2.19 Uppercase **T**

Trace and write.

$\mathcal{T}$ $\mathcal{T}$ $\mathcal{T}$ $\mathcal{T}$ $\mathcal{T}$

$\mathcal{Te}$ $\mathcal{Te}$ $\mathcal{Te}$ $\mathcal{Te}$ $\mathcal{Te}$

$\mathcal{Tr}$ $\mathcal{Tr}$ $\mathcal{Tr}$ $\mathcal{Tr}$ $\mathcal{Tr}$

$\mathcal{To}$ $\mathcal{To}$ $\mathcal{To}$ $\mathcal{To}$ $\mathcal{To}$

$\mathcal{Ta}$ $\mathcal{Ta}$ $\mathcal{Ta}$ $\mathcal{Th}$ $\mathcal{Th}$

Lesson 2.20   Uppercase **F**

Trace and write.

F   *F*   *F*   *F*   *F*

Fo   *Fo*   *Fo*   *Fo*   *Fo*

Fl   *Fl*   *Fl*   *Fl*   *Fl*

Fr   *Fr*   *Fr*   *Fr*   *Fr*

Fi   *Fi*   *Fe*   *Fe*   *Fe*

Lesson 2.21   Uppercase **I**

Trace and write.

Lesson 2.22 Uppercase **J**

Trace and write.

J J J J J

Ja Ja Ja Ja Ja

Jo Jo Jo Jo Jo

Ju Ju Ju Ju Ju

Je Je Je Je Je

NAME _____

Uppercase **T**, **F**, **I**, and **J**

Trace and write.

Turkey

Finland

Illinois

July

Lesson 2.23　Uppercase **D**

Trace and write.

$\mathcal{D}$ $\mathcal{D}$ $\mathcal{D}$ $\mathcal{D}$ $\mathcal{D}$

$\mathcal{Da}$ $\mathcal{Da}$ $\mathcal{Da}$ $\mathcal{Da}$ $\mathcal{Da}$

$\mathcal{Do}$ $\mathcal{Do}$ $\mathcal{Do}$ $\mathcal{Do}$ $\mathcal{Do}$

$\mathcal{Di}$ $\mathcal{Di}$ $\mathcal{Di}$ $\mathcal{Di}$ $\mathcal{Di}$

$\mathcal{De}$ $\mathcal{De}$ $\mathcal{De}$ $\mathcal{De}$ $\mathcal{De}$

Lesson 2.24 Uppercase **L**

Trace and write.

Lesson 2.25 Uppercase **G**

Trace and write.

G   *G*   *G*   *G*   *G*

Ge   *Ge*   *Ge*   *Ge*   *Ge*

Go   *Go*   *Go*   *Go*   *Go*

Gr   *Gr*   *Gr*   *Gr*   *Gr*

Ga   *Ga*   *Ga*   *Gu*   *Gu*

Lesson 2.26 Uppercase **S**

Trace and write.

$\mathcal{S}$ $\mathcal{S}$ $\mathcal{S}$ $\mathcal{S}$ $\mathcal{S}$

$\mathcal{St}$ $\mathcal{St}$ $\mathcal{St}$ $\mathcal{St}$ $\mathcal{St}$

$\mathcal{Sm}$ $\mathcal{Sm}$ $\mathcal{Sm}$ $\mathcal{Sm}$

$\mathcal{St}$ $\mathcal{St}$ $\mathcal{St}$ $\mathcal{St}$ $\mathcal{St}$

$\mathcal{So}$ $\mathcal{So}$ $\mathcal{So}$ $\mathcal{So}$ $\mathcal{So}$

Review Lessons 2.23–2.26   Uppercase **D**, **L**, **G**, and **S**

Trace and write.

David

Ling

Greece

Saturn

Trace and write.

algebra

centimeter

cylinder

division

eighth

Lesson 3.1　Math Words

Trace and write.

factor

fifth

geometry

hexagon

kilometer

Lesson 3.1 Math Words

Trace and write.

multiplication

ordinal

parallelogram

quadrilateral

rhombus

Lesson 3.1   Math Words

Trace and write.

square

symmetrical

thousandth

width

volume

Lesson 3.2   Language Arts Words

Trace and write.

abbreviation

antonym

apostrophe

capitalize

conjunction

Lesson 3.2   Language Arts Words

Trace and write.

dialogue

exclamation

homograph

idiom

imagery

Lesson 3.2 Language Arts Words

Trace and write.

literature

metaphor

onomatopoeia

persuasive

possessive

Lesson 3.2   Language Arts Words

Trace and write.

quotation

rhythm

sequence

simile

voice

Lesson 3.3 Science Words

Trace and write.

adapt

biodiversity

circuit

earthquake

erosion

Lesson 3.3　Science Words

Trace and write.

glacier

gravity

inherit

insulator

landform

Lesson 3.3   Science Words

Trace and write.

magnetic

nonliving

orbit

pollution

reproduce

Lesson 3.3   Science Words

Trace and write.

sediment

species

traits

volcanic

wetland

Lesson 3.4   Social Studies Words

Trace and write.

Athens

Colosseum

continent

equator

France

Lesson 3.4 Social Studies Words

Trace and write.

geography

hemisphere

Hungary

isthmus

Lebanon

Lesson 3.4 Social Studies Words

Trace and write.

Massachusetts

New England

Northwest Passage

population

Renaissance

Lesson 3.4 Social Studies Words

Trace and write.

Sparta

transportation

Taiwan

Ukraine

Zaire

Final Review A-Z Sentences

The sentence below uses all letters of the alphabet. Use it to practice your cursive.

Jeff boxed eleven queasy chipmunks to win a prize pig.

Final Review | **A-Z** Sentences

The sentence below uses all letters of the alphabet. Use it to practice your cursive.

Wizened men drink agave juice and chomp flax seed, but quietly.

Final Review **A-Z** Sentences

Write your own sentence that uses the entire alphabet.

_____
- -
_____
- -
_____
- -
_____
- -
_____
- -
_____
- -
_____
- -
_____
- -
_____

Final Test   On Your Own

Write a note to a friend in cursive. Don't forget to sign your name.